Primary Science

for the Caribbean:
an integrated approach

Tony Russell

Book 1

Nelson Thornes Primary Science

Published in 2003 by:
Nelson Thornes Ltd
Delta Place
27 Bath Road
CHELTENHAM
GL53 7TH
United Kingdom

03 04 05 06 07 / 10 9 8 7 6 5 4 3 2 1

A catalogue record for this book is available from the British Library

ISBN 0 7487 6990 0

Illustrations by Jane Bottomley
Page make-up by IFA Design Ltd, Plymouth, UK

Printed in Croatia by Zrinski

Book 1 contents
Theme: All about me and my environment

Acknowledgements

The photographs in this book appear courtesy of David Simson/B-6490 Septon (DASPHOTOGB@aol.com) with the exception of: Digital Vision PB (NT), Photodisc 61 (NT), Corbis V261 (NT), Brendan Byrne/Digital Vision SD (NT) (p. 1); Instant Art Haz (NT) (p. 36).

Who am I?

Look at the pictures.

Find the one most like you.

Why did you choose that one? Tell the class.

Find two **differences** between the children in the pictures.

Talk about them.

When we are born we are small.
- We cannot walk.
- We cannot talk.
- We cannot eat solid food.
- We have no teeth.

Look at the picture.
What are the children doing?
Tell the class.

Activity 1

You will need: string, scissors, pins, paper, a pencil and a book.

1 Take off your shoes. Stand close to the wall.

2 Ask a friend to put a book on your head. Move away from the wall while your friend holds the book still.

3 With a friend, use string to measure your height. Cut the string.

4 Pin your string to the wall. Write your name on a small piece of paper and put it on your string.

Look at all the strings.
Compare them.
What do you see?
Why are they different?

Some children are tall.
Some children are short.

Activity 2

You will need: string, scissors, pins, paper and a pencil.

1 Choose what you will measure in your group.

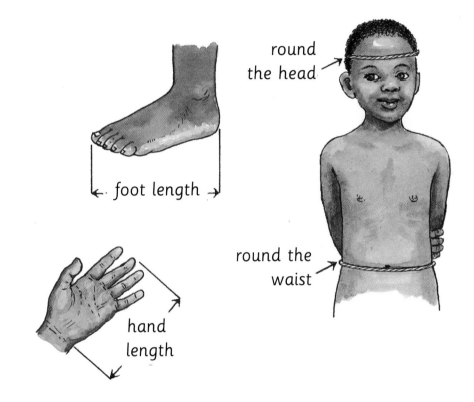

round
the head

foot length

round the
waist

hand
length

2 Use the string to measure the size of the part you chose.

3 Cut the string and put your name on it.

4 Pin it on the wall.

Look at the strings. Compare them.
What do you see?
Why are they different?

Activity 3

You will need: a large sheet of paper, a pencil, scissors and pins.

(1) Put the paper on the floor.
Lie down on the paper.

(2) Let your friend draw round you.

(3) Cut out your picture.

(4) Pin it on the wall. Put your name on it.

Look at all the pictures. Compare them.
What do you see?

Some children have longer legs than others.
Some children have shorter arms than others.
Some children are bigger than others.

Activity 4

You will need: a pencil.

1 Find your **age** on the number line.

2 Put your name on the number line on the wall.

3 How many children in your class are the **same age** as you?

4 How many are younger than you?

5 How many are older than you?

6 Put your age on the picture you made in Activity 3.

Look at the pictures and ages.
What do you see? Tell the class.

Children of the same age are not all the same **height**.

Children of different ages may be the same size.

6

> Look at the pictures.
> Talk about what you can see.

We all belong to **groups**.
Here are the names of some groups:

children **family** **club** **adults** **team** town **church** **school**
class humanity **country** village ethnic group

Your class is a **group**. What is your class called?
Your family is a **group**. What is your family called?

Activity 5

You will need: cards and a pencil.

1 Write your name on a card.
Put it in one group that you belong to.

2 Do this for all the groups you belong to.

3 Look at all the groups. What is the same about all of them?
What is different about them?

We are all human.
We belong to a class and a school.
Not all of us belong to a team or a club.

Some people belong in a village.
Some people belong in a town.

Activity 6

You will need: 15 different objects.

1 Collect 15 different objects. Put them on the desk.

continued over the page

2 Look at each one. Talk about:

- its colour
- its size
- its shape
- what it is made of (**material**)
- what it feels like (**texture**).

3 **Sort** the objects into groups.

4 Look at the groups made by the other children.
Why have they put things in those groups?

5 Tell the class the names of your groups.

Everything belongs to a group.
We can group things by colour.
We can group things by shape.
We can group things by size.
The same thing can be in more than one group.

My body

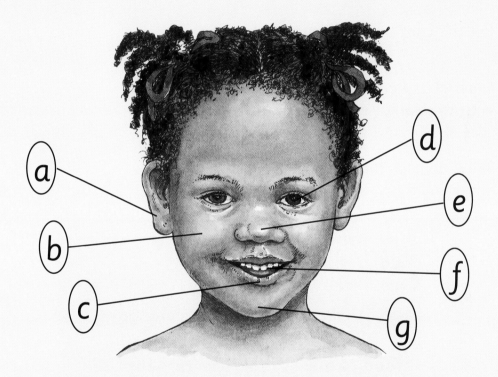

ear eye nose lip mouth

tongue cheek chin

teeth

Look at the picture.

Name all the parts.

Touch each part on your head and name it.

Write down the names of the parts.

Activity 1

You will need: paper and a pencil.

1. Look at the word on the card that your teacher gives you.

2. Touch the part named on the card.

3. Put the card on the drawing of the head.

4. Draw your head.
Put the names of the parts on it.

5. Show your picture to the class.

Copy these sentences.

Use these words to fill in the gaps:

food   ears   speak   teeth   eat   see

We use the parts to do things.
We use our _ _ _ _ to hear sounds.
We use our mouth to _ _ _ _ _ and to _ _ _ and to breathe.
We use our eyes to _ _ _.
We use our _ _ _ _ _ to bite and chew our _ _ _ _.

What do we use the other parts for? Tell the class.

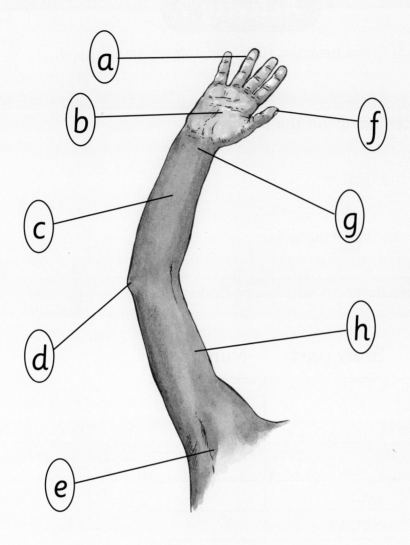

hand   finger   thumb

forearm   elbow   upper arm

armpit   wrist

Look at the picture.

Name all the parts.

Touch each part on your body and name it.

Activity 2

You will need: a pencil, a ruler and some squared paper.

(1) Look at the words on the picture.

(2) Sort out the names.

(3) Put them with the parts.

(4) How many arms do you have? Copy this table:

Body part	Number
arms	2
hands	
fingers	
eyes	
elbows	
ears	
wrists	
nose	
mouth	
lips	
tongue	

(5) Count and write the numbers for each part.

continued opposite

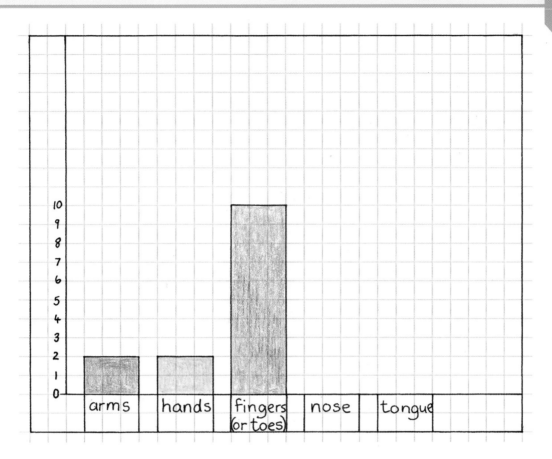

6 Copy this block graph and draw blocks for the parts.

7 Show your graph and say what it shows.

Copy these sentences.

Use these words, and one word of your choice, to fill in the gaps:

hand   nose   tongue   five

We have only one _ _ _ _ and one _ _ _ _ _ _ _.
We have two _ _ _ _ _ _ _ _ _ _ _ _.
We have _ _ _ _ fingers on each _ _ _ _.

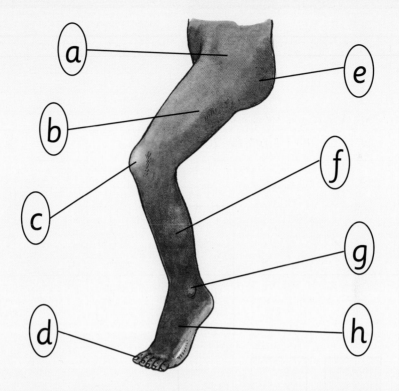

Look at this picture.

Touch each part on your body and name it.

ankle   foot   knee   hip   thigh   shin   toe   bottom

Activity 3

You will need: paper and a pencil.

(1) Draw pictures to show what you can do with some parts of your body.

(2) Write the name of each part on the drawings.

(3) Show them to the class.

continued opposite

How many ways can you make **percussion** sounds using body parts?

Show the class what you can do.
'Play' your body as you sing or say a **rhyme**.

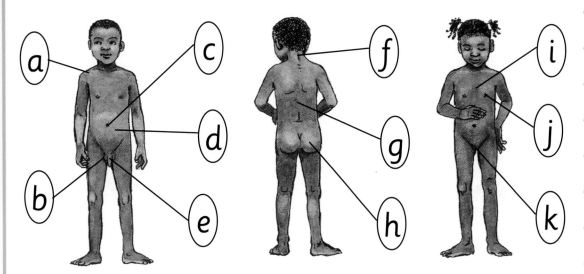

**chest   shoulder   neck   belly   bottom   back   navel
nipple   penis   scrotum   vulva**

Look at the pictures.
What do you call each part?
Tell the class.

Name the parts using the words under the pictures.
Which picture shows a girl?   How do you know?
Which picture shows a boy? How do you know?

Human beings are of two genders.
They are male or female.

Girls and women are female.
Boys and men are male.

Which gender are you?

Activity 4

You will need: paper and a pencil.

(1) Draw a picture of a girl or a boy.

(2) Put the names of the body parts on the drawing.

(3) Use your drawing in a play about girls and boys.

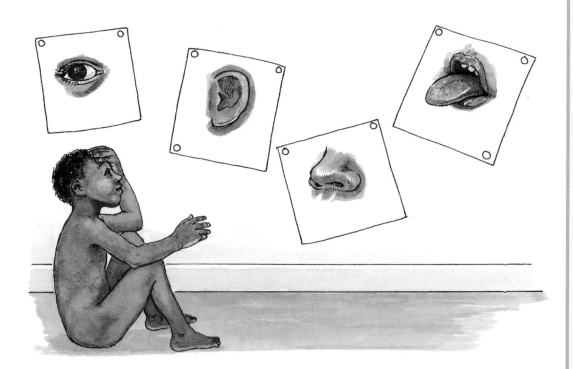

Name the parts in the pictures.

The whole body is covered with _ _ _ _.
The eyes, ears, nose, tongue and skin all do special work.
They are called the **sense organs**.
They tell us about the world around us.

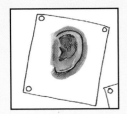

Sense organ	Sense
eyes	touch
ears	smell
nose	sight
tongue	hearing
skin	taste

Copy the words shown above.

Draw lines to match the senses to the sense organs.

The first one has been done for you.

Activity 5

You will need: an outdoor area where you can walk.

Go on a nature walk. Try to use all your senses.

Look at the children in the picture.

Which senses are they using?

Activity 6

You will need: five different objects and a **blindfold**.

1   Cover your eyes.

2   Use your senses to name the **object**.

3   Use your senses to tell the **shape**.

4   Use your senses to tell the **material**.

5   Use your senses to tell the **texture**.

6   Can you tell the colour? Why?

Our senses work together to tell us many things about the world.

Life is more difficult if we do not have all five senses.

Activity 7

You will need: a mirror.

1   Open your mouth wide.

2   Use the mirror to see inside your mouth.
Point to these parts:
tongue   teeth   lips.

3   Close your mouth.
What can you see now?

4   Make your face show:
● eating sweet food
● eating sour food
● eating salty food.
Show the class.

Activity 8

You will need: paint, paper and a paint tray or a plate.

1. Make some footprints, as shown.

2. Make some handprints, as shown.

3. You could do this at home too.

4. You could **print** on card and cloth too.

Activity 9

You will need: a pencil.

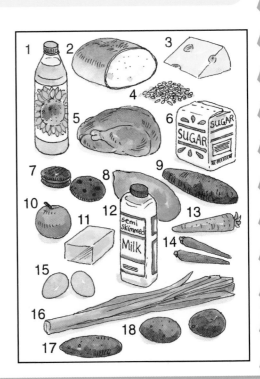

1. Look at the **foods** in the picture.

2. Name them all.

3. Put the foods into **sets**.
   Write the numbers in the
   sets you make.

4. Tell the class about your sets.

5. Draw some of your sets.

Foods are of different kinds.

Some come
from plants.

Some come from
animals.

We need foods to
help us **grow**.

We need foods to help
our body do its **work**.

We need some foods to keep
us strong and **healthy**.

Activity 10

You will need: different foods or packets.

1. Sort the foods and packets into three sets:
   - foods for growth
   - foods for work
   - foods for health.

2. Write a list of the foods in each set.

3. Each time you eat a food at home or school put an X next to it.

4. At the end of the week add the Xs for each food.

5. Which food did you eat most often? Is this good?
   Tell the class.

Copy these sentences.
Use these words to fill the spaces:

food   nuts   grow   plants   meat   healthy   animals   good

1 Fruits and _ _ _ _ come from _ _ _ _ _ _.

2 Milk and _ _ _ _ come from _ _ _ _ _ _ _.

3 My body needs foods to _ _ _ _, work and be _ _ _ _ _ _ _.

4 It is _ _ _ _ to have different kinds of _ _ _ _.

Look at this picture.
Act like these children.
Why are they different?

Listen to the story about being
healthy that your teacher tells you.

What other things do we need to grow and be healthy?
Tell the class.
This picture will help you.

Write a list of the things we need.

Look at these pictures.
What are these things all used for?

Activity 11

You will need: a ruler or straight stick, string or thread, two small lids/pots of the same size, small stone, sand and seeds.

1. Tie the string in the middle of the stick.

2. Hold the string and let the stick **balance**.

3. Hang a lid/pot on each end of the stick.

4. Put a stone in one lid/pot.
   Add sand to the other lid/pot until the stick is balanced.
   What can you say about the **mass** of the stone?

5. Do this again using seeds, not sand.
   What can you say about the mass of the seeds?

6. Use your balance to compare the masses of other things.

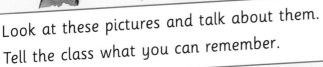

Look at these pictures and talk about them.
Tell the class what you can remember.

Activity 12

You will need: bathroom scales, tape measure/metre stick,
stones and a bucket.

1. Take off your shoes. Stand by the wall.
   Get a friend to mark how tall you are.

2. **Measure** the **height** using your **hand span**.
   Write it down.

3. Measure your height using the tape measure or metre stick.
   Write it down.

4. Stand on the scales. Read your **mass**.
   Write it down.

5. Put a bucket on the scales.
   Put stones in it until the mass is the same as yours.

6. Count how many stones are in the bucket.
   Write the number down.

As we get older we grow.
We get **taller**. Our height **increases**.
We get **heavier**. Our mass **increases**.

Look at this picture.

What do you use these things for?

Tell the class.

Write their names in a chart.

Why do we need to use them?

Tell the class.

Activity 13

You will need: a doll, a bowl, a towel, a comb, soap and a toothbrush.

1   Use the doll to show how to take care of your body.

2   Talk about what you do.

To care for our bodies we must keep them **clean.**
We must also keep them **safe**.
Many places are **dangerous**.
Name some **unsafe** places around you.
Name some safe places around you.

Many things are dangerous.
Name some dangerous things.

Look at this picture.
Find the dangerous things.
Tell the class.

We must take care when we play **outside**.
Which senses do we use?

We must take care when we play inside too.
Accidents can happen at home.
Talk about keeping safe at home.

Look at this picture.
Find the dangerous things.
Tell the class.

Make rules about putting things in safe places.

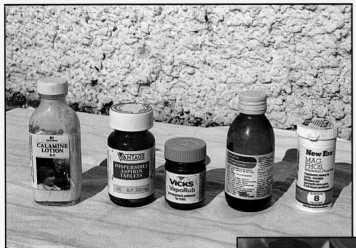

Medicines are good.
They help us when we are sick.

Medicines are also **dangerous**.
If we take too much we can die.

If we take the wrong medicine we can die.

How can we keep medicines safely?
Tell the class.

Act out a scene to show what you think.

These things are also dangerous.

They can kill us.

Where should they be put to keep us safe?

Activity 14

You will need: a **fire extinguisher**

(1) Make the sound of an **ambulance**.
Make the sound of a **fire engine**.

(2) Why do they make those sounds?
What do they tell us?
Tell the class.

(3) Look at the **fire extinguisher**.
Listen to the rules about
how it is used.

Term 2 Unit 1

My family

Activity 1

You will need: drawing paper and coloured pencils or crayons.

1. Draw your family.
   Do not forget to draw yourself.

2. Write the names on the drawing.

3. Tell the class about your drawing.

4. Write some words or sentences about your family.

Look at this picture.
What is the family doing?

Is your family the same as this one?
How does your family differ from
this one?

Sing songs about the family.

Look at these pictures.

Tell the class what you see in each picture.

We all need these things.
They are our **basic needs**.
We cannot live without them.
Our family gives us these things.
We need our family.

Activity 2

You will need: a space **outside** where you can run around.

1 Go outside for some **exercise**.

2 Run, jump, and move your arms and legs up and down.

3 Go back to class and rest.

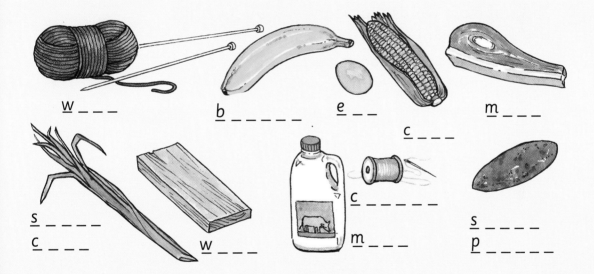

w _ _ _   b _ _ _ _ _ _   e _ _   m _ _ _

c _ _ _

s _ _ _ _ _   c _ _ _ _ _ _   s _ _ _ _

c _ _ _   w _ _ _   m _ _ _   p _ _ _ _ _

Look at these pictures.

Which things come from plants?

Which things come from animals?

Complete the names.

Write them down.

Our family needs to use plants and animals.
Some are used for food.

What do we use others for?

Tell the class.

Activity 3

You will need: a pencil, paper and word book.

1. Write the names of the things in the pictures.
   Put words in sets with the same first letter.

2. Think of more words that start with these letters.
   Use the names of plants and animals.
   Use the names of our basic needs.

Term 2 Unit 2

Things in the home

Look at this picture.

What are the children doing?

What are the sets?

Sort the other things into the sets.

Tell the class what you have done.

Activity 4

You will need: drawing paper and a pencil.

1. Fold the paper in half.
   Write 'natural' at the top of one half.
   Write 'man-made' at the top of the other half.

2. Draw a man-made thing in your home. Name it.

3. Draw a natural thing in your home. Name it.

4. Add more things to your sets. Name them all.

Look at this picture.

Find all the sound makers. Name them.

Which sounds are **loud**? Which sounds are **soft**?

Which sounds are **high pitched**? Which sounds are **low pitched**?

Which sounds do you like? Which sounds do you not like?

Activity 5

> You will need: a tape recorder and tape of sounds, instruments and sound makers.

1. Listen to the sounds on the tape. Name each one.

2. Use your hands to show high/low.
   Use your hands to show loud/soft.
   Use your hands to show sounds you like/do not like.

3. Use your body (voice, hands) to make sounds like those you heard on the tape.

4. Use instruments and other sound makers to make sounds you hear at home.

Look at this picture.

Look for the **dangerous** things.

Tell the class what you find.

What can happen if you play with these things?

Your parents tell you not to play with dangerous
things at home.
They warn you. They want you to be safe.
Some things have a **warning** on them.

Have you seen warnings like these?

Tell the class why they are used.

We can have safety rules.

They can help to keep us **safe**.

Look at these pictures.

Find the animals and the plants.

What are the people doing?

Tell the class.

Activity 6

You will need: drawing paper and colouring materials.

1. Draw a picture to show how you care for plants or animals at home.

2. Write a sentence under the picture.

3. Put the picture in the Big Book.

Children at school care for plants and animals.

You can help take care of plants and animals.

Keep a **record** every day of what you do.

Ezekiel Stoneman	
date	what I did today
2nd October	I watered the plant
3rd October	

Draw a **table** like this one.

Write in it every time you do some caring.

Term **3** Unit **1**

How do I know my school?

This picture shows a sounds game.

How do you play it?

Tell the class what you think.

Activity 1

You will need: a **blindfold**, two or more instruments or other sound makers (keys, whistle, tambourine, etc.)

(1) Sit in a circle. Blindfold one person.
This person sits in the centre, as in the picture opposite.

(2) Make a sound when your teacher points at you.

(3) Did the person in the centre point at you?
Did they name the sound?

In the game you did two things:
• you pointed to the **direction** from which the sound came
• you named the **source** of the sound.

Now do the same two things again.

Activity 2

(1) Sit with your eyes closed.
Listen carefully to all the sounds around you.

(2) Try to work out the source of each sound.

(3) Try to work out the direction of each sound.

continued opposite

4 Try to work out if the sound is made **inside** or **outside** the room.

5 Tell the class about the sounds you have heard.

Look at this picture.

Did you hear the sound of any of these things?

Activity 3

You will need: four different instruments, four other sound makers and a screen.

1 Play the game 'What is that sound?'
Take turns to use one of the things to make a sound from behind the screen.

2 Ask the class to name the sound.

continued over the page

3 Now change the sound:
- make it longer or shorter
- make it lower or higher
- make it louder or softer
- make it faster or slower.

4 Ask the class to say how the sound has changed.

5 Move your hands to show the changes in the sounds.

We use our ears to hear sounds.
There are many different sounds.
We can name many sources of sound.
We can often tell the direction of a sound.
We can hear when sounds change.
Sounds can be loud, high, short and slow.
Sounds can also be soft, low, long and fast.

Word list

accident	something which you do not mean to happen (like a car crash)
age	how many months and years you have lived
ambulance	carries sick and injured people to hospital
balance	to make it stay level (not up or down on one side)
basic needs	the things we must have to stay alive
blindfold	a cover over the eyes that stops us seeing (a cloth or mask)
clean	washed, not dirty
compare	find out what is different and what is the same
dangerous	not safe, harmful, can hurt
differences	things which are not the same
direction	the way something comes (from the front, from behind, from the left or right)
ethnic group	people who share common features
exercise	making the body work to keep it fit and strong
fire engine	a machine that carries water and ladders to fight fires
fire extinguisher	a tool used to put out fires
foods	the things we eat to keep us alive
group	a number of people with some things in common
grow	to get bigger, taller, fatter
handspan	the distance from the thumb to little finger when the hand is spread open
healthy	not sick or ill; being well
heavier	weighs more, has more mass
height	how tall you are, from the top of your head to the ground
high pitch	sounds above, up from another sound, higher in a scale
humanity	all the people in the world
increases	becomes more, gets bigger

inside	in the house, school or other building
loud	a big noise, easy to hear
low pitch	sounds below, down from another sound, lower in a scale
mass	the amount of material (stuff) in an object
material	what something is made of, the stuff, the substance
measure	to find out the size
medicines	drugs that help to make us well when we are sick
object	thing
outside	in the open, not in a building
percussion	sounds made by hitting something
print	make a mark by pressing
record	writing or drawings of what was done or what has happened
rhyme	a short song or poem
safe	not being hurt, damaged, harmed; out of danger
same	having common features, not different
sense organs	special parts of the body that tell us what is happening
set	a group of things with something in common
shape	what a thing looks like
soft	a small noise, hard to hear
sort	put into groups
source	place where something comes from
table	a way of writing things down in rows and columns
taller	has a greater height
texture	what a thing feels like (e.g. rough, smooth, hard, sticky, soft, silky)
town	a place with lots of people and houses
unsafe	dangerous, harmful, damaging, can hurt us
village	a place with a small group of houses in the country
warning	a notice that tells us to be careful because there is danger
work	to move, lift, carry